ABOUT THE METRIC SYSTEM

By Alma Gilleo

Illustrated by Nancy Inderieden

ELGIN, ILLINOIS 60120

This book is designed to be used AFTER the four other books in the series. The other books discuss and provide experiences in measuring linear distance, volume, weight, and temperature. This book provides a review of all these subjects. It gives an overview of the entire Metric System.

The purposes of this book are as follows:

- to give a short history of how measuring units developed and changed;
- to show how the Metric System works, how the units of measurement are related;
- to review what students have learned about the various Metric units.

You will need these materials (Most were used in the other books.):

- meter tapes or sticks (may be homemade, see *About Meters*);
- paper, pencils;
- objects to measure;
- gram weights;
- liter containers (may be homemade, from quart milk cartons).

Distributed by Childrens Press, 1224 West Van Buren Street, Chicago, Illinois 60607.

Library of Congress Cataloging in Publication Data

Gilleo, Alma, 1920-
    About the metric system.

    "A Metric book."
    SUMMARY: An introduction to the development of the metric system and the metric units for measuring length, weight, volume, and temperature.
    1. Metric system—Juvenile literature. [1. Metric system] I. Inderieden, Nancy. II. Title.
QC92.5.G53   389'.152   77-23253
ISBN 0-913778-88-5

Hello. I'm Jake, the lion tamer at the Metric Circus. I used to be a school teacher. Now I teach my daughter, Julie. And, of course, I train my lions.

A long, long time ago, people used parts of their bodies to measure things. These parts were their <u>units of measurement</u> (u - nits of meas - ure - ment).

They used fingers to measure small things.

Sometimes, they used a hand.

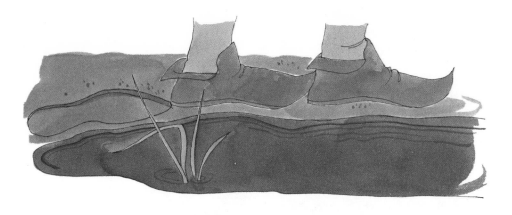

They used their feet to measure, too.

And they used the length of an arm. With an arm length, they could measure large objects.

Using parts of the body to measure things caused problems. One man's foot was longer than another man's foot.

One person's arm was shorter than another person's arm.

Then along came a king in England. He thought of a way to make measuring easy. Some people think he used parts of his body to make patterns. These became <u>units</u> <u>of</u> <u>measurement</u>.

The length of his foot was called 1 foot.

The length of his arm was another unit. (He measured from the tips of his fingers to the tip of his nose.) It was called 1 yard.

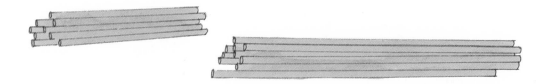

Measuring sticks were made from the king's patterns. Each 1-foot measuring stick, or ruler, was the same length. Each 1-yard measuring stick was the same length.

So people stopped using their own feet and arms to measure things. Instead, they used the new measuring sticks.

In other countries, people used other ways to measure things. A man in France thought of a new way to measure. His way was easy. But people did not use it much.

Many years passed. Then some other men from France remembered his idea. They used it to make a new measuring system. They called their new plan the <u>Metric</u> <u>System</u> (met - ric sys - tem).

The <u>Metric System</u> is easy to use. So, in most of the world, people use it. In the United States, a measuring system made up of feet, pounds, and quarts has been used. It is not as easy. Soon the United States will use the Metric System.

Can you count to 10 or 100? If you can, you can use this plan.

Have you heard of a <u>meter</u> (me - ter)? A <u>meter</u> is one unit of measurement in the Metric System.

Many things can be measured with the <u>meter</u>. A meter can tell how tall or how wide. It can tell how long or how far. A short way to write meter is **m**.

Get a 1-meter tape or a 1-meter stick. Measure things in your room.

In a meter, there are 10 units. Each of these units is called a <u>decimeter</u> (dec - i - me - ter). A <u>decimeter</u> is this long.

——————————————————————

Ten <u>decimeters</u> make 1 meter. Use a <u>decimeter</u> to measure things that are shorter than 1 meter.

Get a strip of paper. Place the strip of paper along the red line above. With a pencil, mark where the line begins and where it ends. Cut your paper on the marks you made. Now you have a paper strip that is 1 decimeter long.

Use your strip to measure things in your room.

There is a short way to write decimeter. Use the symbol **dm.**

You know there are 10 units in a meter. Each is a decimeter. Well, there are also 10 units in a deci-meter. Each one is called a <u>centimeter</u> (cen - ti - me - ter).

A <u>centimeter</u> is used to measure small things.

Make a <u>centimeter</u> ruler. Just mark in the <u>centime-ters</u> on your decimeter strip.

Use your centimeter ruler to measure things in your room. How many centimeters long is a new crayon? How long is your pencil?

A short way to write centimeter is **cm.**

Do you think a centimeter is small? Well, there is something smaller. There are 10 units in a centimeter. See how tiny they are?

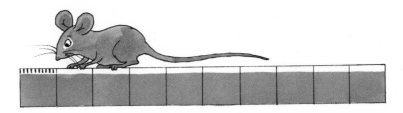

Each of these units is called a <u>millimeter</u> (mil - li - me - ter). A short way to write <u>millimeter</u> is **mm.**

Do you want to measure something tiny? Measure it with <u>millimeters</u>.

An ant is little. Mark <u>millimeters</u> on your decimeter strip. Then measure the ants in the picture. How many millimeters long are they?

What other little things can you measure?

Now you know how to measure little things. But could you measure wide things? Could you measure your playground?

That is easy. Just add meters together. Ten meters in a row are as long as 1 <u>dekameter</u> (dek - a - me - ter). You could use <u>dekameters</u> to measure your playground.

There is a short way to write <u>dekameter</u>. Use the symbol **dam**.

Someday, you might want to measure something really big. You might want to know how big a farm is. To find out, you would add dekameters together. Ten dekameters are as long as 1 <u>hectometer</u> (hec - to - me - ter).

There is a short way to write <u>hectometer</u>. The symbol is **hm**.

A farm is big. But what if you wanted to measure something even bigger? You might need to know the distance to another city. What would you use to measure? You would use <u>kilometers</u> (kil - o - me - ters). There are 10 hectometers in 1 <u>kilometer</u>.

The short way to write <u>kilometer</u> is **km**.

Many units measure how long, how far, how wide, or how tall. Here are some of them.

10 millimeters (**mm**) = 1 centimeter (**cm**)
10 centimeters (**cm**) = 1 decimeter (**dm**)
10 decimeters (**dm**) = 1 meter (**m**)
10 meters (**m**) = 1 dekameter (**dam**)
10 dekameters (**dam**) = 1 hectometer (**hm**)
10 hectometers (**hm**) = 1 kilometer (**km**)

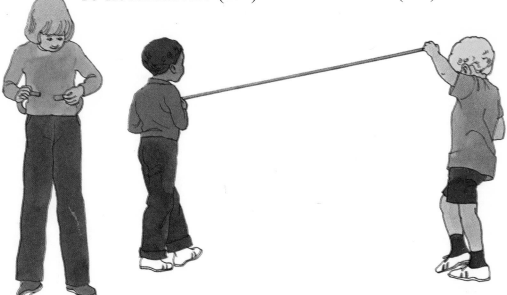

You know you can measure long and wide with the Metric System. You can also measure how much things weigh.

A <u>gram</u> is a unit to measure weight. Some small things weigh about 1 <u>gram</u>.

Two paper clips weigh about 1 <u>gram</u>.

Find other things that weigh about 1 <u>gram</u>.

Find things that weigh 2 grams.

The symbol for gram is **g**.

To weigh still smaller things, use the <u>decigram</u> (dec -
i - gram). Ten <u>decigrams</u> weigh the same as 1 gram.

Two drops of water weigh about 1 <u>decigram</u>.

There is a short way to write <u>decigram</u>. Use the
symbol **dg**.

To weigh even tinier things, use the <u>centigram</u>
(cen - ti - gram). Ten <u>centigrams</u> weigh the same as 1
decigram.

There is a short way to write <u>centigram</u>. Use the
symbol **cg**.

For things that are smaller still, use the <u>milligram</u>.
The symbol is **mg**.

Some things are heavier than 1 gram. Do you know how to weigh them? Just add grams together.

Ten grams weigh the same as 1 <u>dekagram</u>.

Two nickels weigh about 1 <u>dekagram</u>.

There is an easy way to write <u>dekagram</u>. Use the symbol **dag**.

Do you want to weigh something still heavier? Use hectograms (hec - to - grams). Ten dekagrams weigh the same as 1 hectogram.

You can use the short way to write hectogram. It is the symbol **hg**.

How many things can you find that weigh more than 1 hectogram?

How much does each thing weigh?

Make a chart showing things you weigh.

A <u>kilogram</u> (kil - o - gram) is the unit to weigh heavy objects. Can you guess how much a <u>kilogram</u> weighs? Yes. It weighs the same as 10 hectograms.

A short way to write <u>kilogram</u> is **kg**.

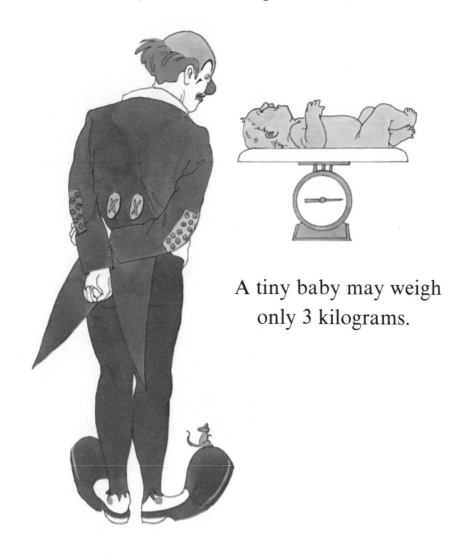

A tiny baby may weigh only 3 kilograms.

Hobo, our clown, weighs 79 kilograms.
How many kilograms do you weigh?

Here is a list of units of measurement. You can use them to measure how much things weigh.

10 milligrams (**mg**) = 1 centigram (**cg**)
10 centigrams (**cg**) = 1 decigram (**dg**)
10 decigrams (**dg**) = 1 gram (**g**)
10 grams (**g**) = 1 dekagram (**dag**)
10 dekagrams (**dag**) = 1 hectogram (**hg**)
10 hectograms (**hg**) = 1 kilogram (**kg**)

Some time, you might want to know how much something holds. <u>Volume</u> (vol - ume) means how much something holds. To measure <u>volume</u>, you could use the <u>liter</u> (li - ter).

A milk carton like this holds almost 1 <u>liter</u>.

A short way to write <u>liter</u> is **l**.

You might want to measure less than 1 liter. If you do, use <u>deciliters</u> (dec - i - li - ters). Ten <u>deciliters</u> hold the same as 1 liter.

Can you guess the symbol for <u>deciliter</u>? It is **dl**.

A smaller unit is the <u>centiliter</u> (cen - ti - li - ter). Ten <u>centiliters</u> hold the same as 1 deciliter.

Two teaspoons will hold about 1 <u>centiliter</u>.

The symbol for <u>centiliter</u> is **cl**.

An even smaller unit is the <u>milliliter</u> (mil - li - li - ter). One milliliter is about two drops of water. That is small!

The symbol for <u>milliliter</u> is **ml**.

These units measure volume.

10 milliliters (**ml**) = 1 centiliter (**cl**)
10 centiliters (**cl**) = 1 deciliter (**dl**)
10 deciliters (**dl**) = 1 liter (**l**)
10 liters (**l**) = 1 dekaliter (**dal**)
10 dekaliters (**dal**) = 1 hectoliter (**hl**)
10 hectoliters (**hl**) = 1 kiloliter (**kl**)

Do you want to measure heat and cold? Use the Celsius <u>thermometer</u> (ther - mom - e - ter). It is also called the <u>Centigrade</u> thermometer, because it is divided into 100 degrees between freezing and boiling.

At 100°, water boils.

Your normal body <u>temperature</u> (tem - per - a - ture) is about 37°.

A room might be between 20° and 25°.

At 0°, water freezes.

Now, look again at all the Metric words for linear measurements and for measuring weight and volume.

Look at the beginnings of the words. Which ones are alike?

Look at the endings of the words. Which ones are alike?

Does that make it easier to figure out the Metric System?

10 milliliters (**ml**) = 1 centiliter (**cl**)
10 centiliters (**cl**) = 1 deciliter (**dl**)
10 deciliters (**dl**) = 1 liter (**l**)
10 liters (**l**) = 1 dekaliter (**dal**)
10 dekaliters (**dal**) = 1 hectoliter (**hl**)
10 hectoliters (**hl**) = 1 kiloliter (**kl**)

10 milligrams (**mg**) = 1 centigram (**cg**)
10 centigrams (**cg**) = 1 decigram (**dg**)
10 decigrams (**dg**) = 1 gram (**g**)
10 grams (**g**) = 1 dekagram (**dag**)
10 dekagrams (**dag**) = 1 hectogram (**hg**)
10 hectograms (**hg**) = 1 kilogram (**kg**)

10 millimeters (**mm**) = 1 centimeter (**cm**)
10 centimeters (**cm**) = 1 decimeter (**dm**)
10 decimeters (**dm**) = 1 meter (**m**)
10 meters (**m**) = 1 dekameter (**dam**)
10 dekameters (**dam**) = 1 hectometer (**hm**)
10 hectometers (**hm**) = 1 kilometer (**km**)

Also, look again at the Metric measurement for heat and cold.

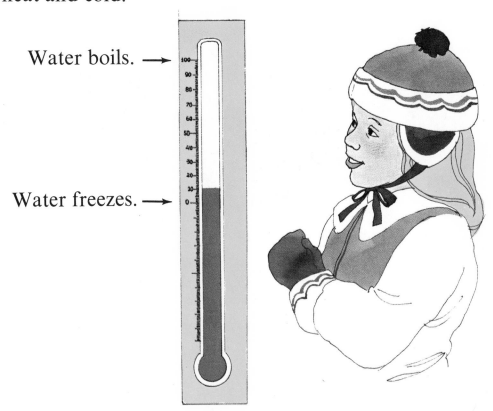

Water boils. →

Water freezes. →

Celsius or Centigrade Thermometer

So now you know about the Metric System. You can measure almost anything with it.

You can measure how high or how wide.

You can measure how long or how far.

You can find out how much something weighs.

You can find out how much something holds.

You can even measure how hot and how cold things are.

Have fun measuring!